Second Person

# Second Person

Rata Gordon

Victoria University of Wellington Press

Victoria University of Wellington Press
PO Box 600 Wellington
New Zealand
vup.wgtn.ac.nz

ISBN 9781776563067


Printed by Ligare, Auckland

'Oh, my beautiful, wonderful disaster.'

— Tove Jansson, *The Fillyjonk Who Believed in Disasters*

# Contents

*iii*

*iv*

*i*

# The pregnant pioneer looks over her shoulder

I'm dressed in yellow leaking
gorse seeds out my pockets like
crumbs I am dressed in white skin
drinking from the spout of a
teapot the Waikato is
clear and twisting onto my
tongue rats are roaming under
my skirt my son is sprouting
legs like a tadpole a tree
falls a tree falls a tree falls
sparrows flap from my armpits
spiders crawl on my sweaty
nape the main issue we have
is mud

# Being born

There was black moss
and a black doris
plum (my head)

I slipped out
on the carpet
my skin was red

*She has a nice little*
*penis*
my sister said

*Umbilical cord*
said my mother
through sweat

Black mushrooms
bloomed
under the bed

# Thumb in a house

Pinching flakes for gold
fish. Two piglets nose
my palm. Pink cheeks in
the light of a hut.
Bamboo poles and sheets
with pansies and holes.

Blue rope swing: a stick
to sit on. Dust up
my nose when a car
speeds past. A red streak
in our dog's fur where
the neighbour shot her.

Polar bears live in
the toilet's white ice.
Rabbits as big as
your thumb in a house
boat floating in the
hall. The cat ate my
mouse, and a fantail

swam through the window
to say our granddad
has gone somewhere else.
Warm pyjamas
by the fire. A sip
of rain before bed.

# Stone

It landed in my mother's underwear drawer
in a rimu box with a fitted lid
the one where she keeps my teeth

She tells me a moa traipsed it
around the lip
of the Hokianga harbour

It was in the moa's gut
grinding fern roots and becoming
smoother and smaller

At the Tasman Sea
she opened her beak
her eyelids closed upwards

I ask if one day
the stone might smash
through the bedroom window

to start a new life
as the tooth in a statue
of an open-mouthed queen

but she says
the stone knows better than to leap
while we are watching

## 14

Our house was cut in half with a chainsaw
and moved onto the paddock by truck.
Fourteen ducklings sat on my knee
to watch TV, and shat on the carpet.
We got a new fireplace, and I
wanted to watch the fire all night.
But she still wanted to watch TV.
I painted sonnets on the wallpaper
and a yellow and lilac bee.
The next week I ripped it down.
Honey on Weetbix for breakfast.
Then I painted the walls brown.
The slice went through my bedroom
and never properly got stitched up.

# Hair

There is plenty of hair, don't worry about that. I have hair on my chin like a billy goat, hair in my eyebrows, hair between my teeth and coming out my nose. Hair on my hands, and between my fingers.

Hair around my belly button to guard against someone who might want to be my mother, and attach to me umbilically. Hair down there, down there, in there and out of there.

We were only small and under the table, and there was all our hair. I gave her a power fringe, she gave me a mullet.

Younger, when Mum cut my fingernails for the first time (they're a kind of hair) my sister screamed and yelped for me *No! You can't throw those away, they're hers!* My tiny crescent moons, flicked into the garden.

Older, I liked to scrape my fingernails through the rotting wood on the deck, just for the pleasure of cleaning them again.

We would peel the tiny white hairs off mandarins with our fingers and undress the fruit of its inner skin. Take out the segments one by one, and eat them. One time, we used tweezers to do it.

Now I use the tweezers, the same ones, to pluck the young man from my face, to pluck away the billy goat, get off, get out of my shadow. I am a woman now, bare, bare, bare. I am a woman now, with hair.

# I find slaters

If I write about trees
I have to write about everything –

blue cheese and pink grapefruit.
A small gold bell ringing over moss.
Politicians' billboards discarded on the side of the road.

I like hating people.
It is fun.
Dolphin-killers and men in tall buildings with snuffly noses.
Men who are rifling through my emails.

I am rifling through this poem
trying to find
its hidden meaning.
If I rifle through fallen leaves
I find slaters.

The leaves are being digested.

How much twiddling do trees do?
Do they doodle on the sky?
Do they do a little spiral?

I didn't mean what I said
about hating people.

That tree is a taraire.
If it could
it would hold a sign saying
*I'm an individual.*

It is breathing in the air
my hot water bottle breathed out.

A small gold bell is ringing over moss.
The leaves are being digested.
The poem is eating itself.

# Dust house

my sister is humming
through wallpaper
the front door is shutting
and opening like lungs
to kauri trees
leaping upwards through air
my lungs are pressed
between walls
grey warblers sing like
dust moving through air
the sunflower is opening
and shutting like lungs
my lungs are shifting
the air

# Wall

You could paint the yellow
shapes that the sun makes
on the wall. Light a cigarette
and burn holes in the wallpaper.
Lots of holes. In the shape of Jesus
or an albatross.

You could install a line of power sockets
along the top of the wall and plug in all your
appliances, and they could hang down the wall like
limp patients. Or you could hang seaweed from the top.

Smear clay on the wall. Or cake mixture.
Pop coloured bubbles on the wall. Dip your whole body in
ink like a Chinese fish and slap yourself against it.

Run and jump at it and make shoulder-shaped grooves and
then pick through the gib with your fingernails. Rip the
wallpaper down, and into shreds.

Throw handfuls of flour. Mix the flour with water and paint
it on the wall and then throw turmeric, and it will stick.
Make moulds of your teeth from plaster of Paris and then
videotape them chomping through the gib, and it will make
a chalky sound.

Nail pieces of firewood to the wall and climb them, or have
a series of pipes coming out of the wall. Train a snake to slip
around them. You can throw cups at the wall. New cups or

old cups. Some of the pieces of cup might stay in the wall if you throw them hard enough.

Cut shapes in the wall, through to the kitchen. Square, circle, star, heart. Practise throwing toast through the holes. Buttons. Olives with their pits in. Train a wax-eye to fly through. Or a swallow.

Fill the holes with potting mix and plant strawberries inside. Go into the garden, pick the chrysalises off the swan plant, and Sellotape them to the wall in a line. The butterflies will spring out like magician's silk.

You can cause the wall to vibrate very gently by sitting in front of it on a chair and playing the cello.

## Small town

dogs in pain
on freshly cut grass
chewing gum and tarseal
in my belly button
cars diving into cold water
Barbie dolls walking barefoot
between peonies
their plastic feet
their stinking exhaust fumes
they make the toilet dirty
just like the rest of us
a bottle top has lost its mother
an ant has a headache
now the Barbies have plastic liver cancer
and speak in hoarse whispers
let's clothe the road-workers in clean sheets
let's feed the grass
some burnt toast

# Where to go

I am considering blowing my nose
in Buenos Aires or perhaps

going to Guangzhou to think
about my bank balance.

There is the option
of mulling on my father's

faults at Fort Myers, or feeling guilty
about my Nana in Nagpur.

I could go to New York
to catch a yellow

flower in the footpath
or be surprised by a cat

in Dharamsala. I might like to feel
an ant on my inner arm

in Amsterdam, or find a nipple
to suck in Nepal. Maybe

there's a black-and-white bird
in Antarctica which will

turn its head in my direction
and I'll feel fine gravel like a toothbrush

under my thumb.

*ii*

# Varanasi

a dog
barking in the dark
at the fish that flickers

through his own
    wet heart

## Vagator

A hot room is slowly leaning in.
A monsoon is arriving on heavy legs.

Tension is burrowed in the lengths of my arms.
It has something to do with being naked.

Not the naked of that woman's body made of lumps of flesh trying to
    escape each other.
Naked in a quiet way.

The way this girl appears beside me in my wealthy sleep and asks me
    for my water.
She gulps it back.

Is it me who is embarrassed?
Is the sea embarrassed at its weight?

Inside it are slops of cow poo, plastic bottles and thousands of years
    of dust –
flaked off, stood on, casually kissed by thousands of humans' skin.

I am not naked in the water.
My cuts and grazes gape to the universes that swirl there.

This is not a competition.
A monsoon is arriving on wounded legs.

# Dharamsala slugs

In Auckland
your small grey
mouth cheapened
my lettuce leaves
but here

you're a thick
and fearless tongue
The right side of my
brain has snuck out
my ear

and gone
wandering
and glistening
It's raining and
you're tasting
the path

I keep
telling you his
tongue was in some
woman's ear but you
are not listening
You're too

busy licking
all the things we
secretly suspected
were holy

# Mango

In Delhi the dust
gets up your nose and into
your veins it swims
through the insides
of your bones

In April you want to hurt
yourself in the hotel room
but you don't because a mango
will make it better

You walk through the streets
in second person as if
watching yourself from behind
your backpack and your hands
are limp but your heart is
beating

This is all you have
to look forward to
your heartbeat and a
mango
everything else has dissolved:
your family
your intentions

There are directions this story could take
to the Taj Mahal
back home to Grey Lynn
to the end of your life

but time does not move
so fast here

You have only taken two steps outside
and somebody has pushed your
body from behind
you feel like a maggot
in a rotting sheep
and the image is comforting

All the other maggots pressed together
chewing through the meat like
synchronised swimmers
all you want
is to not be alone

To not be alone in the hotel room
with the man who thinks
he loves you
but who appears to you with
a sheep's head
and soft knees
when you imagine him
in the dark

The mango
the thing to sink your teeth into
the way to get from this moment to the next
it is reeling you down the road like a fishing line
each jandalled footstep sending puffs of dust between
your toes

You feel sorry
you have not done more
with this moment
you have not caught someone's eye
or let a dance open your body
like an umbrella in the street

You arrive at the fruit stall
and press your left hand around
one cold mango
you lift it to show the man
what you want

# The sun was an axe

and my nipples were flaking onions
and my upper lip was a scaled fish
and my tongue was a pair of scissors jammed in thick canvas
and my knees were half-grown chickens dodging motorbikes on
    the road
and my forehead was a dragonfly caught in the grill of a truck
and my breasts were sacks of plastic bottles carried by skinny boys
and my husband was diesel exhaust fumes
and my uterus was a blackened pot

## In her pants

an inkling
                a tickle
                        a trickle


                                a smell in the jam
                                        black rosary


                                keep going they tell him
                even when life has no blows
no jobs and no


                enlightenment even


                                when the best you'll get
                                        is a lump of sugar too big
                                                to carry home


                                        they tell her the time


                                is now


and apart from


                        walking quickly

from her fantasy that


they are soldiers


they have the issue to deal with
of finding a route


into her pants

# Since I last wrote

Came home
with a pile of papers.
Left neat piles of folded things
in the corner of every room.

Feasted on fire,
water,
bread.

Reached into the arms of a baby,
screamed with his screaming,
slept in his arms.

The hippies had fat joints and black eyes,
tattoos tying knots on the skin,
and questions wider than the valley.

Me too.
Like how to write about sex?
And not say *skin* or, worse,

*the confluence of rivers?*
And not destroy the secret of
*si, si, si?*

Walked alone. Was asked
by women to buy
milk for their babies.

Didn't do yoga, didn't make signs
for Smoking Pranayama,
Virtual Yoga, Spoken Massage,
on May 32 and June 0.
Was a fish trapped on land
in the meditation hall.

Took my face to the richest cake.
Pretended there was a beginning,
a middle,
an end.

# Eggs

I took six raw eggs to the lesbian
bar in San Francisco and drank
until I didn't know how
to recognise a quarter
for the bus driver

but the girl with the teeth
had written on a napkin
directions for how to get back
to my bed and I followed them

she had been writing on a napkin
when I sat beside down beside her

we talked about Orlando and our mothers
and wondered whether trees' offspring
remembered what our grandparents had done
to their parents
whether they winced
when we walked by

I told her I wasn't gonna spike her drink
when she covered it with a coaster
before she went to the bathroom
and she said no
that's to let the barman know
not to take it away

I started writing on my own napkin
*I took six raw eggs to the lesbian*
*bar*
when she came back she said
*that's a great start*
it was 1:30am

I told her I had walked past the bar three times
before I worked up the courage to walk in
she asked me where I was staying
I told her my boyfriend wants to open up
our relationship
she said the BART doesn't run this late
I said I have no idea how to get back
to the room where I'm staying
so she wrote
the directions on my napkin

at the bus stop
I was taller
than I expected
I got off at Excelsia and peed
in someone's yard and wrote LOVE
on many frosted windscreens and found
Santa Rosa and did not do up my belt

I found number 1743 with the glowing doorbell
and the key
fit the lock

I ate small cold carrots
with my shoes on
I sent a message to my boyfriend
*Do I need to sign the form*
*in front of a notary public*
and I forgot to put a question
mark and then I

remembered

so I opened the zip
and the lid and the eggs
were all still
intact

they were bigger
than I expected

I moved them
somewhere good
somewhere they would not
get broken

# Why?

So your cells will glow like grapefruit.
So your nose will clear.
So you won't die of a heroin overdose.
So you can wear a magenta kimono to the supermarket.
So you don't have to go to the supermarket.
So the dolphins will swim through the wastewater pipes and
    wait for you in the bath.
So the dust mites will jump out of your bed.
So you can forget that smell.
So you can get a tan on your inner thighs.
So your mouth will fill with gold glitter.
So your armpits will smell like cinnamon.
So they'll never find out where you're hiding.
So you can manifest the Life of Your Dreams.
So everyone will fall in love with you.
So the slugs will come when you call them from the lettuces.
So the blades of grass will bow to you.
So you can sneeze once and for all.
So you can be as loud as you like.
So you don't have to wear false teeth.
So you won't have to hide a rat in your mouth.
So the cracks in the pavement will close.
So the billboards will fold into origami frogs.
So you won't grow an exoskeleton.
So the flies will spell your name on the window.
So you'll never have to wear a concrete dressing gown.
So you'll feel snug like a stitch in a cardigan.

*iii*

# Not seagulls

This is not a poem about seagulls.
It is not about wind sprinting
through pōhutukawa trees or
the sky dripping with tūī or
daisies tripping over themselves.
It is definitely not about pāua shells.

It is not about coming home
or how calm and tender
is the meat of my heart.
Or how the sun who is
my sun and not your sun
is lifting my spirits like
lifting my skirt.

As if I need saving
from the night who is
a man with a hammer
wrapped in a thick blanket.
This poem won't pretend
to be peaceful.

It won't make up smooth
metaphors about sea glass
or work through its sex drive
by smearing pastels
in the shape of testicular cells.
This poem doesn't want therapy.

It doesn't want to open like
a mussel sloshed in hot water
or stink like a fantail with its
foot stuck in a fencepost.

It doesn't want to drink beer
or kombucha or talk about
climate change and
it's not sorry.

It doesn't care about
being a carnivore or a dinosaur or
loving the bathroom door
even though it slammed
on this poem's little finger.

It doesn't want to make a sound.
It won't let rip with a whole screeching flock.
This poem is not about seagulls.

# How I arrived

whale blubber
was strapped across my back
a wad of flesh with dark
grey skin tied on with rope
fraying at the ends
threaded with shells and purple
beads and beady eyes of spiders
looking out like the pitter patter
of piano keys and hanging down my front
were peanuts strung together in copper
wire latticework with small unlit matchsticks
sticking outwards waving in the wind and written
on these matchsticks were affirmations and dictionary
definitions of words including *customary* and *reverence*
the bodice was made of used handkerchiefs and the lasting
impression was of a Victorian housewife washed up on a beach
nibbled and scratched and worn away by sand-hoppers limpets
    and the teeth
of sprats yes I was wearing a great billowing skirt with fat
sanitary pads soaked with the blood of seals and
I was wearing rubber gloves filled with blue
marbles and fish eyes and in my left hand
was a wicker basket full of pears and
library books telling me how to
be good
and in my right hand
was a wet pillowcase on which was printed
a picture of a baby doll
and I was telling it not to burn the toast and not to look men
    in the eye

remember to say thank you to the bus driver and don't buy
    onions in those red mesh bags
because they are bad news for the turtles
I was dangling an umbilical cord which was split in two
one end was an elephant's snout sucking up this new land
and the other end was a vacuum cleaner
sucking the sky
clean

# Pacing

*A deep bow to Neruda*

It so happens I am sick of being a woman.
It happens that I walk into BP stations and supermarkets
greasy, swollen, like a cow made of soap,
losing my way in a field of placentas and pesticides.

The smell of vet clinics makes me retch.
All I want is to hear silence like stars and dew.
All I want is to see no more shopping bags, no sink holes,
no gear sticks, no flat whites, no fallen leaves.

It so happens that I am sick of my teeth and my underwear
and my thirst and my breath.
It so happens I am sick of being a woman.

Still, it would be wonderful
to frighten a barrister with a possum tail,
or push a monk into a swimming pool.
It would be great
to run through the streets with a water pistol filled with milk
shooting at windows until it started to rain.

I don't want to go on chasing my lists,
clutching at mortgages and chia seed smoothies,
wide awake at night,
gnashing at the mosquitoes who are ruining my life,
and rearranging, controlling, flattening the sheets.

I don't want so much uselessness.
I don't want to go on as a panther
pacing a room,
collapsing in grief.

That's why my emails, when they see me coming
with my bloodshot eyes, clutch each other,
and scamper away like breathless mice,
leaving tracks of fine dust leading under the fridge.

It pushes me to certain beaches, to some oily rock pools,
to hostile hillsides that someone's going to subdivide,
to meeting houses that smell like burning rubber,
and certain stormwater pipes thick with sludge.

There are silver invasive fish, and allergenic nuts
spilling from the taps in kitchens that I hate.
There are polystyrene balls,
and billboards that should have been aborted.
There are black plastic bags full of mouldering bread
and used toothpicks, and wet wipes.

I float through it all, with my skin, my diaphragm,
my fury, letting it all slip off me.
I go through malls, and car yards, and public toilets
and ferry terminals and $2 shops with rubber bananas,
stick-on nails, decision dice, grow-your-own boyfriends,
silver wigs and plastic handcuffs
all waiting expectantly.

# But what should I do with Rata Gordon?

Feed it to the cow.
Burn it. Ask it nicely.
Throw it over the fence.
Turn it into chutney.
Turn it off at the wall.
Use the broom.
Use the grater.
Use the axe.
Tell it to your father.
Leave it in the sun to melt.
Lose it in long grass.
Light incense. Hang garlic.
Post it on Facebook. Post it to your sister.
Tie it to a bamboo pole and run through the city waving it.
Rip it off with wax. Sell it on Trademe.
Scrub it. Use ash.
Use vinegar and newspaper.
Arrange sticks on the beach to spell it.
Dismantle it and stack the pieces by the laundry door.
Tie it to a brick and throw it in the lake.
Hum it under your breath.
Strike it with lightning.
Climb a tree and shout it.
Let it walk onto your finger
and put it on a leaf outside.

# Heavenly creatures

dirt is unwanted particles
the way that weeds are unwanted plants
if the particles are wanted
we call it soil

my legs are made of soil
can you see the sponginess
of my thighs?
The way the rain just sinks right in?

it is because I am decomposing
there are creatures walking, rustling
slipping over and in between
the parts of my body –

ribcase
spleen
the small gravelly
bones in my hands

they are carrying me away
piece by piece
to underground cellars
to the mouths of their children

they want me
they want the sunlight I am made of

# The yellow plate

*i*

We are the lucky ones
who get to lay ourselves out
on a plate and see exactly
what we are made of.

Separate each baked bean
with the tip of the knife,
each bean with its particular
shape and history.

Those three together,
that one with a sad little
bubble upon it.

The way the tomato sauce
sinks into holes in the toast
and fills them.

The yellow plate
plainly lit up around it all
like a halo.

*ii*

I have a heart that pings like a bra strap
and sets off a chain reaction.
I do not get up at 5:30 to see the first light
touch the sea.
I do not climb into the dark water.
I drink turmeric tea and grow
new freckles on my knees.
I'm sorry I did not wash my feet.


*iii*

Now it is me lying on the yellow plate
with pink geraniums and red cherries
passionfruit and crushed basil leaves.
My hair is salty
small black chickens are sleeping against my ankles
a dog has its muzzle in my palm.

The plate is on a cake stand.
There is a blue ribbon saying 'Winner'.
Birds are chiming
like Tibetan singing bowls.
Or does it say 'Loser'?
I can't see from where I am lying.

# Physics

*i*

In the night a tidal wave
of preservative 202
washes over &
embalms the island.

The ferns become rubber,
the geckos become
orange jelly lollies,
the lace hanging
from the tōtara is polyester,
the anemones in the rock pool
come from the bargain bin.

Every millimetre is
cold and still.
Peanut butter
in your ear.
Fists gradwrapped.

The only place to find moving life
is to wonder who is wondering

*Do plastic geckos dream?*

*ii*

The shop display looks lovely
to the moon
who smashes the glass and steals
a diamond ring.
She tries to fit it
on her plump & glowing finger
then sends it flying
into the ocean.

*Who would make a ring so fucking small?*


*iii*

Bacteria open their jaws
to bite into an apple
on the kitchen bench.
They break their teeth
& roll away
like glass beads.

The only thing to bring
this frozen world to life
is an imagination.

*Who has one? Do I?*
*Let me check.*

*iv*

Something is moving in the shadows.
A snake
but not physical at all.
It travels through everything
like black rum through a sieve.

Snakes through a sieve.
Snakes through a diamond ring.
Snakes through the children
and the trees.

*Do they see what they move through?*
*Or does it just feel like a boundless bath*
*of jelly too warm to set?*


*v*

Nothingness moving
through stillness.


*vi*

*Where can we possibly go from here?*

It is a question God asks over & over
& over & over & over
& over

The question repeating is
a vibration,
a tickle.
When it happens quickly enough
it becomes a solid thing,
a body
with fingernails and skin.

# Would you let a kākā in your kitchen window?

What if it nibbled your ear?
What if it ruined your life?
What if you couldn't answer its questions
about your asthma inhaler and cans of beans?
What if it begged you to take away the ceiling?
What if you wrenched out the screws and sent
the corrugated iron thundering to the lawn?
What if it was 2am by the time you were done?
Would you share your lager with this kākā?
While the rain fell into your toaster?

What if you found yourself shredding
your bedroom curtains with your razor?
What if this kākā invited its friends?
What if they spoke in a language
you couldn't always understand?
Would you let tōtara sprout up
between the tiles in the bathroom?
And moss consume your couch?

What if you found a family of ferns
crouching under your sink
licking the lid of your dishwashing liquid?
And what if this kākā woke early?
And you hated the sound
of it cleaning its feathers?
But what if the sound of its laughter
made your heart beat faster?
What if your house became thrilling with life?
What if it laid three

warm
white
eggs

in your lap?
And then left in the night
and didn't come back?

Or what if it did?
Would you let this kākā
in your kitchen window?

# A baby

I want to make a baby out of one peach and one prickle.
I want to use the kitchen sponge, sticky rice and a rubber band.
I want to use the coffee grinder.

I want to make a baby out of concrete and a jackhammer.
I want to use the oil on the driveway.
I want to use rainwater, a cigarette butt and a milk bottle.

I want to make a baby out of wet sand and a nappy.
I want use micro-plastics and plasma.
I want to use cockles and cable-ties and chip packets and pipis.

I want the baby to wake up and cry out.
I want the baby to cry out.
I want to make a baby.

## Full stop

The branch came down right where
Kate and Sam had been sleeping with the baby.
It was thick and soft with water,
the slaters were rushing out and in.

We wiped our feet with a towel
climbed back inside our tent
and tried to go back to sleep.

Trees' DNA does not deteriorate as they age.
Ours does –
the outer limbs weaken and fall off
they rattle around inside our cells.
We forget how to digest,
how to be attractive and
reproduce.

I have eggs stacked inside my ovaries like coins.
I spend one each month.
Sometimes it ends up under the artichokes.
It is as big as a full stop.

I have not forgotten about the branches above us
getting heavier with the rain.
You are breathing so deep and slow
it makes me angry.

Perhaps we won't have the chance to deteriorate.
What if we stop living
with all our DNA intact?
You have already passed yours on –
two warm pink bundles sleeping somewhere else.

The end of my sleeping bag is wet,
my face is greasy.
I get out of the tent and climb inside the sea.
It is soft and penetrable
like a rotting log.

# In the evening

The sea is orange.
A dark shape is moving in the kitchen.
Not just any shape but me, this kitchen, and you.

We greet the dust-mites in the rug.
The kale plants are producing all winter.
Little fragments shine out between our teeth.
There is a pile of washing to sleep under.

Small smiles between us.
Agree, agree.
A love heart blinks, daringly obvious, in the corner.
Agree, agree.
Agree, agree.

A soft moth wants to sing its pink little heart out.
It doesn't.
We agree through gritted teeth.
The fire burns over there.

We don't agree.

Stop making generalisations, I tell you.
Be specific.
My nose hairs concentrate.
I am holding on to sand with my fingernails.
There is a molar in the floorboards where I stand to boil the jug.
We save ourselves by letting our voices go deep.

I tell you I am embarrassed by you, please stop reading tarot
in public.
You tell me it's okay, I'm allowed to be embarrassed.

We lick each other.
Our spines are intact.
The sun comes up.

## My carriage

Inside me
is a carriage,
it is drawn by two dark horses.

Yesterday, one horse
the one with grey forehead
got skittish,
his nostrils flared
and he ran in the wrong direction.

The contents of the carriage
spilled into the toilet bowl.

Can we salvage what came out?
This is what they look like, on the cobblestones:

me, in a bonnet
grazed palms
my husband
unscathed
our child
naked.

My husband rights the carriage.
I calm the horse.
We two climb back inside together.

# Tongues of small birds

when the pīpīwharauroa broke its neck
on our kitchen window
the ceremony began

I put it in the fireplace
to keep it from the flies
lit incense above it
to send the spirit off

as soon as the sun came out
I carried it to the back deck
flicked on my camera
and captured its
colour is too bland a word

I felt like the first astronaut
looking back at Earth from outer space –
the blue-green hum
the incomprehensible bending of light

you wanted to cut out its insides
and salt it
I didn't want to watch

I googled pīpīwharauroa
and found the Māori myth
these birds carry a small white stone
all the way from the Solomon Islands to lick
when they get thirsty
I thought of myth as fallacy

archetype and truth and I wondered
where this bird had dropped its stone

in the morning I noticed exactly
the silence in the sky
where its voice was supposed to fit
I couldn't finish my toast

was there a growing pile of pebbles
at Cape Reinga – each one
shiny and smoothed by the tongues
of small birds?
It is terrible but
the following week I found
another one
dead and gleaming
under the same window
I took it straight
to the compost

# Until

I would like this to be a lull
a little lullaby of sweetness but it isn't

I'd like this to be a lullaby where bank accounts
don't leak, where absorbent pads of meat juice don't get elected,
where my poems haven't dried up
like a prune, like a cervix
like a service station on a Sunday when you are lonely
and no one will look you in the eye

I would like to lead you back
into the world of magic, but I can't

I'm washed up like a starfish
waiting for someone to bring me back to life

waiting

for a speck of dust to start growing inside me

it has worked out
in a dreadful sort of way
and it's hanging in my artwork
like carcasses in a butcher shop

the dolphins haven't visited me yet
but something has

something so deep and bottomless and blue
I can't see the end of it

when I drop everything
and feel for it in the dark
there it is

what if I stopped waiting for a sign?
what if I stopped chasing other people's dogs with sticks?

what if my son is sprouting legs inside a grapefruit
in some far off universe
over and over and over again

until

# Space

the first thing to get rid of
is the image of a bomb:

> matter flying outwards
> from a central
> point

it is not an explosion *into* space
there is nothing
outside of it
to explode into

> it is an explosion *of* space

> expanding

all of space

> everywhere

everywhere is the centre
every craggy outcrop

and everywhere is the farthest edge of the universe
every breath

# Celestial bodies

*i*

When you put Saturn in the bath
it floats.
It's true.

*ii*

A teaspoonful of neutron stars
weighs more than all the world's people
curled up together.

Under the sheets
we glow in the dark
but the light we emit is 1000 times
dimmer than we can see with
naked eyes.

*iii*

We are skinny, you and me, and we weigh less
when the moon is directly above our heads.

Our moon is moving away from us
by 3.8cm every year.

Even very small celestial bodies
can have moons.

When an embryo is 3.8cm long
the uterus is the size of a warm grapefruit.


*iv*


It takes over 8 minutes for the sun's light
to land on the moon
bounce off
hit our bedroom wall and splash
onto the whites of your eyes
then leap
into my pupils.

The further away something is
the farther back in time it appears.

The nearest galaxy
looks as it did
when australopithecus hominid children
chewed on tubers and poked
at a fire with sticks.


*v*


Our bodies glow.
All the world's people
are lifted by the moon.
The smell of grapefruit.
A teaspoon full of fires.
Manuka smoke on my teeth.

The whites of the eyes
of the nearest galaxy.
A bath full of zigzag photons.

You are suddenly
close enough
to be in the same moment
as me.


*vi*


When two pieces of the same type of metal
touch in space
they bond and become permanently stuck
together because they cannot tell themselves apart
from each other.

I don't like it
when you fall asleep
on top of me.


*vii*


The coldest part of the universe is on Earth
(in a lab in Massachusetts) and
we live inside the sun.

We live *inside* the sun.

## The pregnant pioneer takes a seat

I am sipping from the lip
of a huia egg it's
fine like bone china the yolk
slides down my throat my son's
spine is unfurling the ferns are
sniffing the cows whose tails
are curling in spirals the
tūī twist warbles around
the trees it's Sunday I need
to preserve this forest
in a Mason jar yes pickle
the angels then scrub the
potatoes for tea

# Attached

to Earth by my nipples
I am floating above

her small damp mouth
and fierce suck
tether me, stop me
from drifting off

she drinks her sunlight
through me
like a straw

or:

she is attached to Earth
by mouth
her small pink body
flickers like a flag
mouth planted
into the island
of my
breast

# Inhaling

this delicate new day
like the skin of a strawberry
could break and bleed
at any moment

*

the bed is wet concrete
and I am up to my
neck

*

we can do small things
with great love
like
inhaling

*

I want to kick a door down
or break the windscreen of a car
with a sledgehammer or
bite down hard
on the hand
of my significant other

*

the word *breastfeeding* used to be innocuous
like *rubber ball* or *clay*
it has become
a fleshy red
raw heart throb thing
it hurts

*


she falls asleep
she has tunnelled down
from some other universe
to do this one wonderful thing
on me

# A mother

she appears
on page 309
in the Cenozoic age
a live-bearing mammal
who must care for
and suckle her young

the picture shows her
sloping along
tired eyes like prunes

we have recklessly
evolved

now she appears
to be me

apparently mothers' chests
heat up like toaster grills
when their babies are cold
and cool down when their babies
are hot

what is the opposite of a mother?
the grim reaper?

surely not a father

the opposite of mother

        is a space

     as big as the evening sea
             and I am floating in it
     my blood is cool
        like the moon

# Into the midst

isolation is the word burning
a hole in my stomach
even though there is so much
to connect to – look!
a blackbird flying
away from me, hostile
wild strawberries replacing the garden
look! drunk neighbours
calling each other *babe* and
*dickhead*   what a dear world I live in
where the clouds shrink upwards and away
and I am trying to tunnel my way
back into the midst of things
somehow     how do I find the nest
where there are people to touch me
on the upper arm and say *bless you*
when I sneeze?    where
is the place where garden
worms feel friendly rather than
a desolate consolation for
lack of conversation?    here
I am with the fat singing
baby who pulls
my hair       who will let me
pull their hair? on what lovely
giant's back
am I walking?

## Shoreline

In the beginning you
were a grain of sand.

I zoomed in
and you became
the baby.

In the beginning I
was the sea.

You zoomed out
and I became
the mother.

Now we meet
at the seam
skin to skin
eye to eye
on Monday
on the red towel.

The oyster catcher
presses the needle of her beak
down where the sand
is wet.

# Biblioclasm

Those sweaty books that are trying so hard
to say something –
I put them in a pile on the grass.
The day is damp
the clouds are hanging limply like elephant ears.
When I strike the match
the flame deflates and dies
I try again, but no cigar.

Perhaps they will burn better if I shred them first.
I pick one up
a tight-arsed sparrow of a poetry book.
Page 8 it reads:
*Bougainvillea burst through my retina*
I tear the page between burst and through
then hold the match to my retina.
It still won't catch.

Remember sea books? The little fleshy lumps
that wash up at the estuary with 4 pages of green
and a yellowy tail stretching down:
the beginning of a mangrove tree.

Last weekend I went swimming amongst the mangroves
in the Kaipara harbour.
I climbed up the branches
in the water jungle
where no words could find me.

# Notes and Acknowledgements

p. 5: 'Oh, my beautiful, wonderful disaster' is uttered by the Fillyjonk in *Tales from Moominvalley* by Tove Jansson (Avon Books, 1963).

p.66: 'Space' borrows from the words of cosmologist Wendy Freedman: 'The first thing to get rid of is an image analogous to a bomb—which is our first tendency to imagine, and which is wrong—where you have an explosion with matter that flies outward from a center. This is not what happens in space . . .' Quoted by Corey S. Powell, 'Could the Big Bang be Wrong?', *Discover Magazine*, 16 June 2019.

My thanks to the editors of the following publications, where some of these poems first appeared: *Landfall, JAAM, Sweet Mammalian, Geometry, Sport, Food Court, Fast Fibres, Deep South, 4th Floor, blackmail press, Poetry New Zealand Yearbook, Takahē, NZ Poetry Shelf, Convergence, Otago Daily Times, Atlanta Review,* & *brief.*

Thanks to the team at VUP: Fergus Barrowman, Kirsten McDougall, Craig Gamble, Jasmine Sargent, Kyleigh Hodgson and especially Ashleigh Young, who gave many of these poems the haircut they needed.

Some of these poems began their lives as exercise pieces when I was studying a Diploma of Creative Writing through Whitireia New Zealand. Thanks to my classmates, and poetry tutors Lynn Jenner and Samiha Radcliffe for your encouragement.

Other poems were written as part of my Arts Therapy Masters research project titled *Dreaming with my Body: Expressive Arts Therapy, Arts-Based Research and New Motherhood.* Thanks to my research supervisor Deborah Green at Whitecliffe College for being there to catch some of these poems as they came out.

Thank you to the companions who have sat and written alongside me over the last few years, especially Rosie, Aaron, Serena, Amber. Many of these poems wouldn't have made it to the page without you.

Thank you to the other creative families that feel me: my Open Floor family, my improv family, my soul families, blood families, families of animals, insects and microbes, and especially to my home family. Thank you to Ben, my love, who helped to shape many of these poems, and to Ursula, who I adore.